secrets

AF624467

rosalie sherlock

BookLeaf Publishing

secrets © 2021 rosalie sherlock

All rights reserved.

No part of this publication may be reproduced, stored in a retrieval system, or transmitted, in any form or by any means, electronic, mechanical, photocopying, recording or otherwise, without the prior written permission of the presenters.

rosalie sherlock asserts the moral right to be identified as author of this work.

Presentation by *BookLeaf Publishing*

Web: www.bookleafpub.com

E-mail: info@bookleafpub.com

ISBN: 9789357445658

First edition 2021

DEDICATION

to my parents, who have probably heard each of these a hundred times.

secrets

the hallways promised
not to tell,
even though
they saw everything.
the hand holds.
the blushes.
the passing of notes.
what we had,
was our little secret.
until it wasn't.
and then,
our world
came crumbling down.
all around us.

liar

love,
i never thought
it could be right.

in my mind,
it was transitory.
nothing but bad,
no matter the circumstance.

now, the dawn has come.
and i've realized.
your mind doesn't always.
tell the truth.

bittersweet

the coffee that burned my tongue,
when we first locked eyes,
across the cafe.
was almost as bitter,
as our love would be.
i just didn't know it yet.

invisible walls

we build walls for many reasons,
to protect, to hide, to divide different regions

but walls aren't always physical.
it's not always the sticks and stones that build.
the walls that are invisible,
are the ones that are most fulfilled.

we build these walls unknowingly,
to protect ourselves from the outside.
solely because the ones locked out,
don't agree with our pride.

together we march in unity,
for one month a year.
never once were the generations before us given
this opportunity.
the opportunity to express ourselves without
fear.

fear of hatred,
fear of rejection,
fear of ostracism,
fear of pain,
fear of abandonment,

fear of death.

fears that a teenager shouldn’t have to worry
about,
not when their minds are already so plagued
with doubt.
fears that should never cross a child's mind,
they shouldn’t be forced to leave their childhood
behind.
to these internal battles they should be oblivious,
these debilitating fears shouldn’t exist.

yet they do,
and so the building of these invisible walls
ensue.

thank you

to those
who told us
that we could
thank you

to those
who told us
that we couldn't
f*** you

my heaven

i never thought.
i would choose,
hell over heaven.

but if your love.
means, that the time i spend living
is indistinguishable from,
a life after death
in the vast blue sky.

then i'd say it worth it

the better

sometimes,
i do miss you.
but not as much
as i used too.
because remember,
i wished you
the best.
but i wish myself
the better.

chromosomes

i wish i didn't live in a world,
where people tell you,
you can't love someone.
over something as simple,
as you both having x's.

tired

“why are you always so tired?”

at that question,
came the smiled she admired.

“because,
the stars love hearing about you,
but they only come out at night,
so i have to make do.”

risking it all

by simply touching you,
i risk so much.
but it is the meeting,
of our lips,
and the love i feel,
from looking in your eyes.
that tells me it is worth it.

the in-between

the top of a curve, the yellow line
the location of a person's spine
all in the middle,
the in-between.
a societal riddle,
it's who we've always been.

no-one is perfect, it's practically impossible.
even the thought of it isn't plausible.

from the outside and in, we are discriminated
against,
leaving our shoulders permanently tensed.

even the most outward and loving community
has treated us disreputably

we don't conform,
we can't "pick a side"
we get it, you've told us, we can't, we've tried

no, i'm not a girl.
no, i'm not a boy.
and no, i don't have to pick one side to find joy.

why can’t you accept us for who we are
we’re still your friends, your children, we aren’t
that bizarre.

just let us be in the in-between,
if you do, we'll be the happiest you’ve ever seen.

constellations

the ones i've drawn on your back.
don't match the ones in the sky.
the one's that we stare at,
when the sky goes dark,
tell the stories of another.

the one's we've drawn,
tell ours.

face to face

people don’t realize.
how bad,
things can be
for us,
until they’ve come
face to face.

fool

the world fooled me.
into thinking love,
was monstrous.

how on earth,
did i fall for it?

acceptance

i’ve dealt with my refusal of self,
for far too long.
i will not deal with,
your refusal of me too.

rumors

i have a secret,
but you can't tell anyone.
with a solemn nod our eyes connected.
she held out her pinky.
and interlocked it with mine.

i told her everything.
about that girl.
the one commanded my thoughts,
day and night.

so when that secret spread,
i prayed that it wasn't her.
but when she walked into english class.
with a cast on the hand,
she had cast that promise on.

i knew i was wrong.

ethereal

even though,
i planned every moment.
i could never have planned,
how free i would feel.

in orbit

you’re my moon.
and i’m your earth.

two people,
designed as one.

although separated by an atmosphere,
still drawn towards their other half.

the universe sees it too.
maybe one day,
it’ll bring us together,
and never let us drift apart.

hide n' seek

every single time,
i played hide n' seek,
i found myself hiding in the same place.

after i had memorized every article of clothing.
that was so neatly put away.
i realized.

this game went on,
for a lot longer than i thought.

an ode to my younger self

oh child,
i applaud you
in all aspects of life.

oh child, you are brave.
everything that comes your way,
you handle with a grace and beauty.

oh child, you are strong.
when someone pushes you down,
you always stand right back up.

oh child, you are so loved.
never forget that nothing can change,
the way your family loves you.

oh child, i'm proud of you.
proud that you made it this far.
proud that you kept pushing forward.
proud that you are letting yourself be you.

ily

it felt forbidden.
and even though i knew it wasn't.
my mind still told me was a crime.

maybe it was,
the world surrounding.
maybe it was,
the religious grounding.

still,
my soul will live.
forever stained.
by the beautiful moment.
those three words created.

www.ingramcontent.com/pod-product-compliance
Lightning Source LLC
Chambersburg PA
CBHW051720130826
49812CB00034B/1276
9789357445658